4/99

PLAYTALES

PUSS-IN-BOOTS

MOIRA BUTTERFIELD

Heinemann Interactive Library
Des Plaines, Illinois

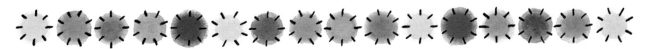

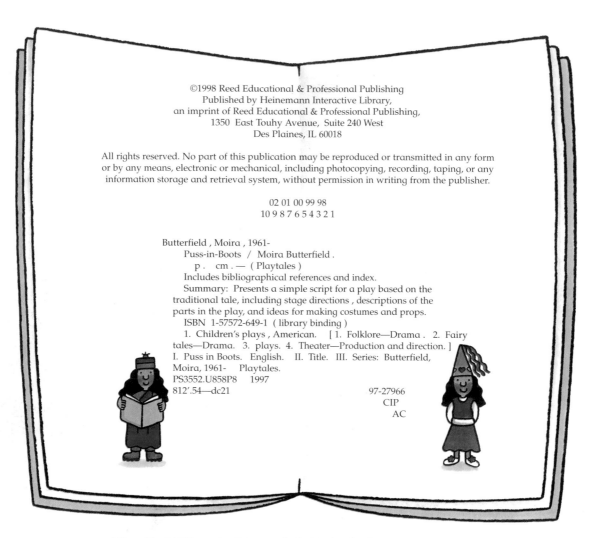

©1998 Reed Educational & Professional Publishing
Published by Heinemann Interactive Library,
an imprint of Reed Educational & Professional Publishing,
1350 East Touhy Avenue, Suite 240 West
Des Plaines, IL 60018

02 01 00 99 98
10 9 8 7 6 5 4 3 2 1

Butterfield , Moira , 1961-
    Puss-in-Boots / Moira Butterfield .
      p .   cm . — (Playtales)
    Includes bibliographical references and index.
    Summary: Presents a simple script for a play based on the
traditional tale, including stage directions , descriptions of the
parts in the play, and ideas for making costumes and props.
    ISBN 1-57572-649-1 (library binding)
    1. Children's plays , American.   [1. Folklore—Drama . 2. Fairy
tales—Drama. 3. plays. 4. Theater—Production and direction.]
I. Puss in Boots. English.   II. Title. III. Series: Butterfield,
Moira, 1961-   Playtales.
PS3552.U858P8   1997
812'.54—dc21
                                                97-27966
                                                   CIP
                                                   AC

Editor: David Riley • Art Director: Cathy Tincknell • Designer: Anne Sharples
Photography: Trever Clifford • Illustrator: Sue Cony • Props: Anne Sharples

Thanks to: Rose Arkell, Joseph Timms, George Suttie,
Juliet Taylor and Yasmina Kahouadji

Printed and bound in Italy

You will need to use scissors and glue to make the props for
your play. Always make sure an adult is there to help you.

Use only water-based face paints and makeup. Children with
sensitive skin should use makeup and face paints with caution.

Contents

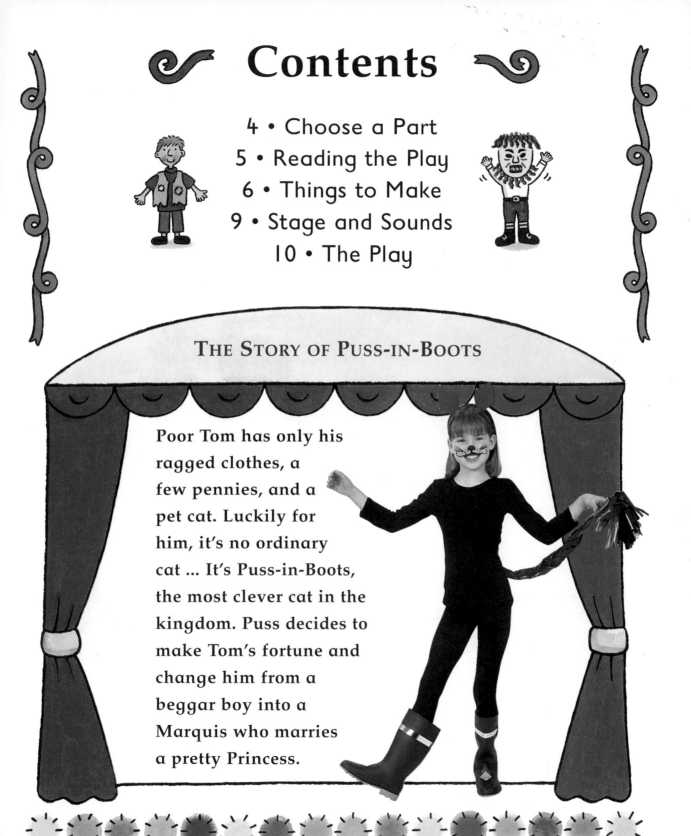

THE STORY OF PUSS-IN-BOOTS

Poor Tom has only his ragged clothes, a few pennies, and a pet cat. Luckily for him, it's no ordinary cat ... It's Puss-in-Boots, the most clever cat in the kingdom. Puss decides to make Tom's fortune and change him from a beggar boy into a Marquis who marries a pretty Princess.

Choose a Part

This play is a story that you can read with your friends and perhaps even act out in front of an audience. You need up to four people. Before you start, choose which parts you would like to play.

These two parts can be played by one person.

King
A very noble man.

Ogre
An ugly giant.

Puss-in-Boots
A clever cat.

Tom
A kind boy.

These two parts can be played by one person.

Storyteller
Someone who helps to tell the tale.

Princess Rose
A pretty young lady.

How many people are going to take part?

If there are four people taking part, sit together so that you can all see the book.

If there are two or three people, divide the parts between you.

If you want to read the play on your own, use a different sounding voice for each part.

Reading the Play

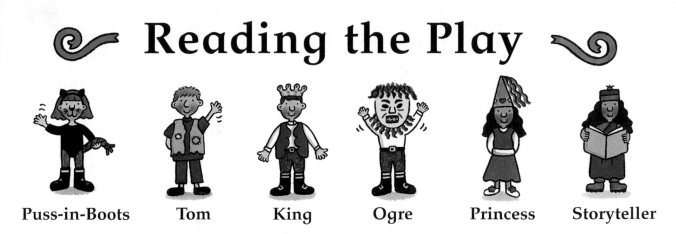

Puss-in-Boots   **Tom**   **King**   **Ogre**   **Princess**   **Storyteller**

The play is made up of different lines. Next to each line there is a name and a picture. This shows who should be talking.

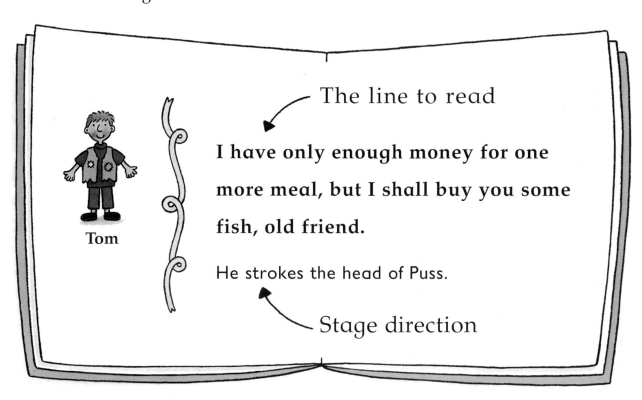

The line to read

I have only enough money for one more meal, but I shall buy you some fish, old friend.

Tom

He strokes the head of Puss.

Stage direction

In between the lines, there are some stage directions. They are suggestions for things you might do, such as, making a noise or acting something out.

Things to Make

Here are some suggestions
for costumes.

TOM: CLOTHES AND PROPS

Tom starts off poor. Wear sneakers and pants and an untucked T-shirt under a ragged vest. Then swap it for a grand vest, and tuck your pants into shiny decorated boots.

Make a Ragged Vest

You need:

- Stiff paper
- Scissors, pencil, and ruler
- Tape or glue
- A T-shirt

1. Cut out three pieces of paper to make your vest. Use your T-shirt as a pattern.

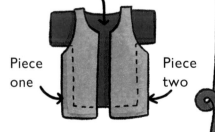

Front of T-shirt

Piece one

Piece two

Back of T-shirt

Piece three

2. Tape or glue the pieces together as shown.

3. Cut around the edges to make the vest look ragged. Draw or stick some patches on.

Make Fancy Boots

You need:

- A pair of rain boots
- Aluminum foil
- Tape
- Scissors

Tape a line of aluminum foil around the top of your boots, and stick buckle-shape pieces on the front .

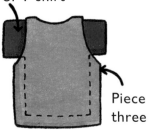

Make a Grand Vest

Follow the ragged vest instructions, but cut three different-shaped pieces like this:

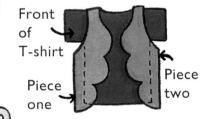

Front of T-shirt

Piece one

Piece two

Back of T-shirt

Back piece

Decorate your grand vest with shiny buttons and scrap paper.

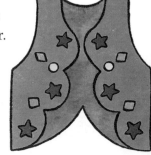

PUSS-IN-BOOTS: CLOTHES AND PROPS

Wear leggings or tights, and a T-shirt, or a leotard, in either gray, black or brown. Use a large safety pin to fasten a tail to the back of your costume, and paint your face like a cat's. Wear shiny decorated rain boots like Tom.

Make a Tail
You need:
- Three strips cut from a trash bag, roughly 20 in. by 4 in.

1. Cut a fringe at the bottom of each strip. Knot the strips together above the fringes.

2. Braid the strips together.

3. Then knot them together near the top and tuck the tail into the back of your belt.

You could twirl your tail around when you speak.

Cut two ears out of stiff black cardboard and tape or glue them on to a head band.

Face Painting Ideas

Put dots and whiskers on your cheeks. Then paint the end of your nose black and put a black line between your nose and your mouth. Make your eyes cat-shaped, if you like.

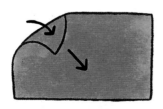 # PRINCESS: CLOTHES AND PROPS
Wear a party dress and a Princess's hat.

Make a Princess's Hat
You need:
- Stiff paper 18 in. by 24 in.
- Tape and scissors
- Ribbons or crepe paper
- Paint or colored paper scraps to decorate the hat

1. Roll the paper down from one corner. Keep rolling to make a cone. Check it fits your head.

2. Tape the cone together and cut around the bottom to make a straight edge.

3. Tape ribbons or strips of crepe paper to the top of the hat, and decorate it any way you like.

KING AND OGRE: CLOTHES AND PROPS

Wear a shirt and pants tucked into decorated boots. The King should wear a crown and a vest like Tom's. The Ogre has a mask to wear.

Make a Crown
You need:
- Shiny thin cardboard
- Scissors, pencil, glue, and tape
- Tape measure and ruler
- Colored paper scraps

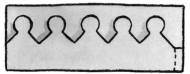

1. Draw a long crown pattern on the back of the cardboard. Make it as wide as you like with points along the top edge. It should be 3 in. longer than the measurement around your head.

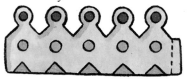

2. Cut out the shape and decorate the front with paper scraps.

3. Tape the two ends together, overlapping them by 1 1/2 in. Check this crown fits before you put the tape on.

Make an Ogre Mask
You need:
- Scrap paper and thin cardboard 8 in. by 10 in.
- Scissors and pencil
- Two pieces of string
- Hole punch
- Paints for decoration

1. Make a practice mask out of scrap paper. Fold the paper in half. Draw half an oval, half a mouth and half a nose shape.

2. Cut out the mask and try it on your face for size. Mark where the eyes should be, and cut them out. Then make the real one from cardboard.

3. Decorate the mask as you like. You could stick lengths of paper around it to make hair and a beard.

4. Punch a hole on either side, just above where your ears should be. Knot the string through the holes so you can tie the lengths in a bow at the back of your head.

Face Painting Ideas
The King could have an elegant beard and mustache.

Stage and Sounds

Once you have read the play through, you may want to perform it in front of an audience. If so, read through this section first. Rehearse the play, working out when you are going to come on and off stage, and what actions you are going to perform.

PROPS

If you like, set up four chairs to represent the inside of the King's coach. Place  two chairs facing the other two chairs.

Have a bag or sack ready as a prop for Puss-in-Boots.

Place a table onstage with a cloth over it to hide underneath. Tom can pretend to swim behind this table.

Actions

Puss-in-Boots should practice twirling his tail and meowing.

The Ogre should practice acting as a lion and as a mouse.

SOUNDS

Practice saying "The Marquis of Carabas". The first word is pronounced Mar-kwis.

If you like, get some assistants to shout offstage as Tom appears to be drowning. Shout things like "Catch him!" and "Pull him out!" You could get someone to make splashing noises by slapping a wooden spoon into a bowl of water.

REHEARSING

Rehearse the play before you ask someone to watch.

The Play

Once upon a time there was a poor boy named Tom. All he had in the world were some ragged clothes, a few pennies, and a pet cat.

The Storyteller points to Tom and Puss, who should stand together.

I am no ordinary cat. I can talk and I can stand up, too!

Puss-in-Boots

3 1833 03412 0425

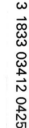

10

Tom

I only have enough money for one more meal, but I shall buy you some fish, old friend.

He strokes the head of Puss.

Puss-in-Boots

Meow. You are a kind boy, Tom, and I'm going to make your fortune. Use your money to buy me a pair of fancy boots and a sack. Don't look so surprised! Just do what I say. Always remember that cats are clever.

Storyteller

Tom did what Puss asked. He bought a sack and some fine boots that fit perfectly.

COSTUME
CHANGE

Puss puts the boots on proudly.

Puss-in-
Boots

I shall call myself Puss-in-Boots from now on.

Storyteller

The cat took Tom to the woods and filled the sack with juicy green leaves.

Puss-in-Boots

Sssh. Keep very quiet, Tom. Hide behind this bush and watch.

If you like, Puss and Tom can pretend to hide behind a door or table and peep out at an open bag.

Storyteller

Soon a rabbit hopped into the bag to eat the leaves. As quick as a flash, Puss pounced on the bag and closed it up.

Puss should pounce on the bag and hold it up.

Puss-in-
Boots

Stay here, Tom. I'm going to take this rabbit to the palace to give to the King. The guards will let me in when they see me in my fine boots.

Puss-in-Boots turns to the King, bows and pretends to hand over the gift.

Puss-in-
Boots

My master, the Marquis of Carabas, sends you this fine rabbit for your supper.

King

Thank you. How very thoughtful.

Storyteller

Then, once again, Puss went to the woods. This time he filled the sack with seeds and caught a fat partridge. He took it to the palace.

Puss bows to the King and pretends to hand over the gift.

Puss-in-Boots

I have another gift from my master, the Marquis of Carabas.

King

Your master is very kind. I'd like to meet him.

Storyteller

Puss-in-Boots told Tom what the King had said.

Tom

My clothes are in rags, Puss. I'll never be allowed through the palace gates.

Puss-in-Boots

Do what I say and you will meet the King. Today, I want you to go swimming under the bridge near the palace.

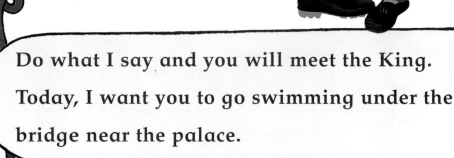

Puss-in-Boots whispers into Tom's ear, as if telling him the rest of a secret plan. Tom should then take off his ragged vest and hide behind a table or door, with his grand vest and boots nearby.

Storyteller

Tom did what his cat asked. He hid his ragged clothes under the bridge, and got into the water. Soon the King's coach came by.

Puss-in-Boots

Help! Help! The Marquis of Carabas is drowning!

King

Stop the coach! Save that man!

Storyteller

The King's soldiers pulled Tom out of the river. They didn't see his old rags hidden on the riverbank.

Tom

All my clothes have been stolen!

King

I'll give you new ones. It's the least I can do. I'm so glad to meet the Marquis of Carabas at last.

COSTUME CHANGE

Tom puts on his grand vest and tucks his pants into his new shiny boots.

Storyteller

Tom and Puss were given a ride in the King's coach. Inside sat the King's daughter, Princess Rose.

COSTUME CHANGE

The Storyteller puts on the Princess's hat.

Princess Rose

Tell me, do you have a castle near here?

Tom

Um, er...

Puss-in-Boots

Of course. It's just down the road. Would you like to have supper there? I shall go and prepare it.

COSTUME CHANGE The person playing the King should take off the crown and put on the Ogre's mask, ready for their other part. The Storyteller takes off the Princess's hat.

Storyteller

Puss-in-Boots jumped from the coach and scampered off to a nearby castle, where he knew a horrible Ogre lived.

Puss-in-Boots

Good day, Ogre. I hear you are quite good at magic.

Ogre

Quite good? How dare you! I'm brilliant!

Watch me turn into a fierce lion who likes eating pussy cats!

Ogre

The Ogre appears to turn into a lion, and chases Puss-in-Boots around, roaring loudly.

I'll bet you can't change into something small, like a mouse.

Puss-in-Boots

The Ogre appears to become a mouse and squeaks. Puss-in-Boots chases him off-stage. Then Puss comes back on stage licking his lips.

I'm good at catching mice. That one was tasty.

Puss-in-Boots

COSTUME
CHANGE

Offstage, the person playing the King should take off the Ogre mask and put the crown back on.

Puss-in-Boots

Ah, here comes the King's coach. Welcome to the castle of the Marquis of Carabas.

Puss-in-Boots
(in a loud whisper to Tom)

Leave everything to me.

Storyteller

The King and the Princess dined on the very best food and drink. Puss-in-Boots had found it all in the Ogre's kitchen.

King

You are obviously very rich, Carabas. Pass me some more caviar, would you?

Puss-in-Boots
(whispers)

Tom, do you like the Princess?

Tom

I love her! Princess, will you marry me?

COSTUME CHANGE

The Storyteller puts on the Princess's hat.

Princess

Yes, dear Marquis.

I loved you from the moment I saw you.

Puss-in-Boots meows and purrs.

23

Tom and the Princess hold hands and parade around with the King and Puss-in-Boots walking behind them in a wedding procession.

Storyteller

Soon there was a wedding, and from that day on, Puss-in-Boots had the best of everything.

Tom

I still don't know how you did it, Puss.

Meow. Remember what I told you. All cats are clever. Meow. Pass me my bowl of cream.

Puss-in-Boots

Puss-in-Boots licks his lips. Then everyone bows to each other or to the audience.